a stranger
to my
purpose

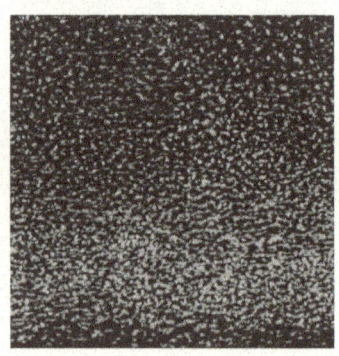

a stranger to my purpose

by
jacob
david
snyder

Acknowledgement is made to the editors of *Anthropocene*, *Eunoia Review*, and *Rising Phoenix Review*, in which some of these poems first appeared.

© 2025 by Jacob David Snyder

All rights reserved. Published by Traveling Companion Publishing, *Publishers since 2020*.

No part of this publication may be reproduced, stored in a retrieval system, or transmitted in any form or by any means, electronic, mechanical, photocopying, recording, or otherwise, or used to train any artificial intelligence technologies, without written permission of the publisher.

This book is a work of fiction. Names, characters, places, and incidents are either the product of the author's imagination or are used fictitiously, and any resemblance to actual persons, living or dead, business establishments, events, or locales is entirely coincidental.

ISBN 979-8-218-73581-4

First printing, September 2025

Cover and interior art by Anagh Banerjee

Cover and interior design by Harry Shapiro

Logo design by Ciara Ní Chuirc

for weil, wales, and the wind

table of contents

act I: ELEGY 1

act II: EFFIGY 13

act III: APOGEE 45

epilogue 67

acknowledgments 71

act I: ELEGY

god speaks in metaphor calls me cardinal calls me lone

moves me by strings springs in my leg arm torso neck crown

sometimes at night i feel them cup my ears many hands no tongues

feel their heat hold me dig canals through me i am the conflux

plough rows across me i am the garden they grow christmas lights

tremble and gasp watching them shine crimson i understand the question

left right yes no i fall down the pachinko machine with the other balls

one day they'll pluck out the pins

it was a suicide

you bought me
for my temperament
declawed and fangless
well-caged
rare beast
i could never
and there are so many
that do

but after a while
you worried for it
needed it
to prove yourself
needed to break flesh
only dreams are painless
declawed and fangless
you gave me
a knife
and told me
to cut

i tried
i tried and tried
but i couldn't pierce you
though i tried and tried
i couldn't go in
incapably tame
impotent
an actor
unable to perform
yet you had your role
chosen before us
reluctant martyr
you took the knife

six inches later
that mortal length

red run cold
though i had tried and tried
i could only watch
tried and tried and tried and
watch, as you
stabbed yourself
turned to me
and asked me
"why"

        * * *

river glides
like glass
if glass crinkled like silk
smells like pine and snow
if pine and snow expanded
outward into
memory

sprigs and buds blotched red
with freshness of their mother
dead though breathing
bark layered like roadwork
urban grid in organic
it feels warm
but it's just my hand
the dead aren't warm

i'm tired of old leaves
though i keep them in my shoes
i press them flat
write between their veins
as they crumble apart
the winter feels
heavier
i stand on the precipice
though i know
i'm already falling

* * *

when i was the protagonist
of my story
resolution pure
scored to the orbits
of our private conceits
per child's tin piccolo
nine pence an odyssey
i always concluded
with a vision of a city
shrouded in luster
and in the light of the last lamppost
cloistered brick
and sighing shrubbery;
there you lay
a picnic prepared
fruit split
upon the cutting board
soup spiced with pepper
sage and thyme, smooth truffles
strands of flaxen squash
rich and tender tenderloin
cabernet
you pour
into a bowl
we share
to drink of each other

now i fear my story
reflects that of my forebearers
my great-uncle wrote it
with the blood of his lungs
hacking typewriter
corner of a sallow cell
arrested for stealing food
with a toy pistol
he knew the collar and the night
knew the skull picked bare
face unremembered
narcissus died despairing

his eyes closed to himself
the city forgets
people of fallow soil
their names husks
we repeat in the dark
as if to conjure
dimming light
vacant noise
on starved lips
indigestible resonance;
i walk the desert desolate
watch for shadows
among the pyres
from vile ash
a casket opens
filled and brimming
with centuries/societies/nobodies
moaning
beckoning
room for one more

* * *

at work
in thought
a post-it note appears
from my pocket
custom printed by
the new york presbyterian health center
your partner in
mental health recovery
it reads:

Before Starting
Clear
History.

i think it's referring
to my computer

* * *

i remember a traveler
you met that night
gangly and earnest
made you laugh when we danced
you asked him outside
where drunkards water stone
"en amérique, est-ce que s'arrêtent-ils
jamais pour regarder les étoiles"
i answered
"je ne me souviens pas des étoiles"

i remember a parisian dog
skinless tail
barking by a shut gate
etched with pawing
fur clumped between
our bodies
his eyes do not know us

i remember a graveyard
where the stones were nameless
as they were
before we named the stars
i kissed you there
beneath the stairway
you tasted like sea foam
perhaps those were tears

* * *

you lent me
le petit prince
in french
and after you had left
that's all i had
left

i read it again now
admitted to isolation's
sanatorium
on the edge of a
singing bowl they pray in lhasa
i read in french and the
circadian rhythm
of the words
put me to
sleep

                                                    wake

                                                                                                 in
                                                                                                 an
                                                                                                 i
                                                                                                 m
                                                                                                 a
                                                                                                 g
                                                                                                 e

                     of the   sahara
           hear you   crying
                                               your plane in pieces
i comfort you   with
     my stories
                         faraway lands
                              eccentric exploits
             but the story you   love most
is
    of
          a
                rose
                      on
                          a
                               shooting
                                       star

you hold out your hands
                                  coarse   and   scarlet
                   "emmène-moi là-bas

                          et je cultiverai un

                          jardin pour toi"

i
touch   your clockwork
                               can't stop   shaking
            this won't last
                                                     only dreams are
                                              painless

               your plane isn't ready
                            and i am lost
                                   in
                                   a
                                   d
                                   e
                                   s
                                   e
                                   r
                                   t

      wake
      snap wake
      like charred ox bone
      and old leaves
      wake in your wake
      the seer that saw her
      and recall your touch
      as if it were my own
      and know
      i must know
      though you're nowhere near
      that what is lost
      can be found

act II: EFFIGY

they hung me here long ago i think in this parlor one of many parallactic taxidermic circus beasts motionless dangling stars and moons and elephants but no light an echelon in aphelion where time is in the womb waiting over cluttered armoires and porcelain cabinets cobwebbed junk indiscernible they left me here for my own good they said they need me to understand but i'll never understand i was meant to be owned i don't understand

years
pass like film
like poppy smoke
lying away from myself
in the middle of empty seats
watching it all happen
forgetting
painless

i'm sorry

*　*　*

perusing over
old photos of us
waterhouse
haenraets
afremov
(vettriano
who liked watching us dance)
our favorite
was edvard munch's
the kiss
aristophanes' androgynous
shared and taken and
fixed

hardest part is seeing you become just another word in this book

* * *

you used to soak
submerge yourself
in water and incense
the fractals of your hair
swirling about you
like the patterns of a place
older than you
where the fields smell
of wind-touched gold
the musk of a bible
long kept though
pages are missing
fields of women
bent beneath
the beating sun
tilling
sowing
harvesting
and you among them
so small
your mother's hands
soaking her flail
with blood
like hers and hers
and hers before
a field of red
and gold

you feared
the empty pot
as much as you feared
its filling
what waited inside
matryoshka
each successive doll
carved open
the rings of a tree
collapsing in on itself
rotting wood

you feared
the end
the center
of the nest
hairless
skinless
cold nothingness of
unborn eyes

* * *

i take shelter
in a blood-black hut
clanking pipes and a narrow stair
buy a lightbulb
but it doesn't fit
i try every lamp
but the lightbulb won't fit
not one socket will take it

and i kick the earth and bellow
"what is your purpose"

* * *

among mattresses
i watch a couple
familiar facade
they purchase a box spring
not looking at each other
silence thick with exhaustion
checkout line
cashier is new
you go to wait in the car
i watch your gait
feel the keys
weigh in my pocket
and only then recall
your face and hands
as i run after you
into the street
thick with exhaust
and scream out
a guttural hoarse sound
that leaves me
sobbing at the edge
of the mattress

why do we play at permanency

* * *

la bohème
i ask for a reading
the room smells
ash and absinthe
flavoring my teeth
her turned-out eye
focused on the windowpane
picks my signifier
fool, and draws
a cross of pale
crooked horsemen
one for each finger
and i laugh
at the cost of it
payments of prophecy
long told

that night i linger
among the crowd in
piazza san marco
watch them flock
pool and course
over marbled glory
bleeding heart of a
skeleton city
arteries overflowing
with unkempt gondolas and
fast fashion gucci
watch them leak in
through the cracks
swell and rise
threatening to
damp the bells

perusing the mannequins
in a shop window
i find one i fancy
proffering me a toy
trade my reading

for a pocket watch
inscribed
"il tempo lo dirà"
later i second act
in a balcony aisle
madama butterfly
terrorful trumpet
the heroine
stabs herself
and i hold the watch
to my ear

at a hostel
huddled by the toilet
i masturbate
into my motherland
clean myself hastily
before walking
to the station platform
never got off

in exile
i am the obscurity
in a windowpane
stained glass piece
dimmed and lost
in the kaleidoscope
of cherished saints
all color rubbed off
by the wet morning
light passes through
unaltered
not even a shadow
on the pews
thus it spreads
over the covenant scene
an ailment taking
the other fragments
their hues lost

to the chapel
where only light shows

i walk alone
through a train
where all sleep
their faces pressed
reflecting against
unwashed windows
as if imprinted on the morning
and in their morning
i see the alps
passing by in procession
indistinguishable and faded
like glass
i see the alps
and know
that even they cannot remain

                              * * *

there are no postcards
where i've been
though i look for them
taste their absence
in a guinness bottle
there is no echo
in this space
between water and firmament
this waiting
nothing remains
but the cathedral
where i saw you
feeding chickens
your face open
and i was the moon
pouring through your window
a child
praying for rain

we were the beast below
primordial, lovecraftian
size and shape
of manhattan submerged
water thick and dark
pulsing through us
and when we passed
our remains surfaced
became the continent
monolith transfigured
from which they grew
and suckled and fed
yet here i lie
a stranger to my purpose
painting our likeness
on eggs

i carry them with me
in a basket
over soft hills

layered with dew
sun veils brush by
caress your face
you break over me
like a peach
wet and sweet
i weep when
finding our old home
i see you carved
my face in your mirror
kept letters unsent
in your jewelry box
folded and organized
by the hour

this i bear
from door to door
asking for those
who saw you
the hills are harder
on my feet
air thick and dark
at sunset i sell my watch
for a crib
sing softly
rocking our eggs
by firelight
the earth inhales

at midnight i
swallow them
like an asp
jaw dislocated
i crush their shells in my throat
feel them slide down
squirming
                      i dreamt
                                we loved in a
                                        walled
                                        garden

```
picked a rose          for you
                                        imbued with     its own glow
                                                           you took it
                 cried out
                                            four thorns
       lodged in            your
                             palm
                             your hand
                             bleeding
over the orchid                 sprigs
                                          i sucked them
          tried to                           pull them
                              with my teeth
     but you didn't stop
                    you kept bleeding
                              you wouldn't


                                               stop


     i wake up
     tasting them
     retch out each one
     breathless, torn open
     i hear them screaming
```

* * *

i sit
in a suitcase
observe planes and persons
behind wrapping plastic
numbered thoughts on a display board
a boy cries in my queue
the aching crowd
baggage check
passport still marked with
your lipstick

you never kissed me at the ocean

i think this in the air
somewhere above
longing and longitude
i'd taken you
who'd never been
you collected shells
smuggled them in my pocket
i cupped the atlantic
and you took it and
baptized me
ANODOS
greek for pathless
ascent

in the chateau's shadow
instrument in picnic
i played arpeggio
triplets in c minor
swam in it
sounded your contours
you smelt like
the spice trade
carried on the breath
of an ancient sea
you sang soprano
a song meant for me

and in that moment
the world
stopped
to listen

years later
positioned before the pews
of a courtroom
judge officiated
blinding cloth
blood on a record
i did not write
i looked for you
but standing in your place
was a woman
i did not know
and in that moment
all the passings of you
like passages of verse
at once and not
real and fiction
untouched words
sung in shadow
a ghost

in george macdonald's phantastes
the protagonist, anodos
pursues a vision
carved from stone
pygmalion's pride
she is ageless
she is unchanging
he pursues her through alder and ash
and at the end of it all
he wakes up

from my plane i look
out the window
observe the great

expanse of blue
i thought i was
watching the ocean
but it turns out i never had

a boy cries in my seat

* * *

my journey over
i return to a land
i once knew
a gift i never did
the earth worn
molded and fired
in grandmother's kiln
its valleys thumb marks
a patchwork quilt
rumpled and creased with use
smelling of her spare room
honking geese in traffic on the riverbank
evergreen hairs on a balding scalp
storms the shade of a ghost story
a road you can't see the end of
a dog affixed to a rocking chair
the porch where you waited

but there is no road
there is no dog
there is no porch

nothing remains

* * *

known many beds
many beds and no sleep
on train tracks and haylofts
in the glow of a kitchen window
insensate satiation
numbing of a pussing wound
all we can carry
crammed in our pockets
no weight but you

san juan
omens inscribed on the tenement
with spray paint and neon
one stripper, rubí
christened for her hair
purred in my ear
"las mujeres nacen de
la espuma del mar"
i starved for her that night

berlin
brauhaus lights greeted me
with a thousand dancers
their cheeks resting in place
of falling snow
each step took me
back to that soft cold albedo
shared between us
our dance in yuletide dark

taipei
i shared eel and drinks
with a slender woman
marketing agent in a hotel bar
a formal affair, utilitarian
first me, then her
turns out anything goes
with enough money and booze
anything can fit

on the welsh coast
i lived out my days
with a divorcée
in the only settlement
her settlement could afford
"mutual agreement"
i took his place
filled the opening
he left behind
and in catharsis comprehend
that though i fill i am not filled
leave again a stranger

i walk a pathway thin and narrow
and hold the space that you occupy
between women and work
between comings and goings
these liminal layovers
canceled flights on broken planes
we are all strangers here

i saw a vision of a city
shrouded in luster
its citizens surround and stare
bathing in its refraction
i told you about this place
long ago i think
we rush there
unrelenting, yearning
discover a dream made of sand
pouring through glass

* * *

```
        sky            an open book
                                                    light its
                                                    scrawling
       all writ
            ten
                to ca

                   scade


                               with
                           gravity
                      filtering through            tree    branches,
                                                           windows, the

membrane           of your  eyelids
                                                    steadily gazing
         from the clouds
                           of your palm
                                                    folding in
                                                              on itself
                                                           alabaster and
                                                              pink
              the light shifts
over our children
                              we remember the future
         shadows           of
echoes
                              we've seen this before
                                   it is a light    we cannot
                                                              read
           the language forgotten
                                   i am an island
in an ocean
                              overflowing
                                                    it spills
                                                              over
          the edge of the bowl
                     pours over the ripples of air
```

                                                                        like
                                                                        lines
                                                                        of
text
the   weight o f threads
            narrowingand
s   p   re   adi   n   g
        gr

                                                o

                w

                                                                                    i

                                        n

g   a   n   d

reducing

with every beat   of your heart

                              * * *

wake among wheat stalks
my harvest lit and breathing
musty summer smell
ripe with rain
a young child plays with pins
in the dirt another
draws on my face hearts
of varying sizes
i watch them
come to me more
running from afar
always near sing
without tongues
stand and they gather
use me to keep
their hands warm
they ask me where
i'm from i tell them
"the between"
they recall it well
i walk north on a whim
and they follow presuming
i cannot last loving
what they'll learn
of me loving
what they'll forget

act III: APOGEE

in chaos shapeless heap clinks clanks of lightning bolts scarred into the hull of the prophetic ark delving through primordial soup i am the product water damaged collecting filled with torrent and tempest they pick me up cast my contents to the storm wash off the remnant i am what lingers skeletal semblance but they do not drop weigh measure throw shatter this hollow vessel there are galaxies in the void they paint my shell crimson raise me so that i may float with the rest suspended above the world their world of possibility

sylvan cove
atop my hill
seismic pines
surround
catch winds
from the west
wisps of winter
shaking, roaring
whispering
i among their coven

as a sapling
i imagined each tree
its own telos
lord and master
the final cause
absolute in its birth
endless in its end
so i aspired
to climb one such tree
and ascend beyond
the atmosphere

now in the darkest of nights
i've finished my climb
and come up short
an end but not the end
disappointed
above the canopy
mauve and brisk
i witness other hilltops
other trees like mine
silhouettes of the form
centuries/societies/everybody
bundled in hooded coats
all pinnacled
all quiet
waiting

"what's happening"
i ask
"wait"
they whisper
nothing, shivering
hear the growing
groaning, creaking
wheels turning
mauve to indigo to marigold
and then
the sun
redder than the thought of red
from which all other
is but imitation
open forge
liquid fire
dripping upward
as if to engulf
the heavens

* * *

the sky leaks
falls
upon the establishment
clouds rolling over
lay splayed
above the sheets

i carry out trash
cans with bare feet
lights turned dim
the greenery glowing
wet
thick with water
my feet burn
on the asphalt
cold that bleeds through
dyes my soles

sparrows in the grass
graze for worms
as i kick off the heads
of dandelions
remember the pattering of rain
on the car roof
like a pot boiling
steaming the windows
i reach over and
feel the passenger seat
still warm

* * *

there is a cage
for all things
for birds and wind and laughter and
a child
snared beneath him
my first owner
between hushed moaning
and the hardwood floor
my pants thrown over my comic book
set aside for later

i hold this in my fist
as i talk to the wall
this cage i
share with him
picked from the earth
his weight the weight of the world
i am the ten-year-old atlas
no countries but lines
drawn across a face
i never washed
entrusted
to carry his people
though my own soles bleed

i am the clown
with the big red nose
and the painted face
he mocks my shoes
he has none
i bow into mud
and play a pig
cheering, claps for encore
i oblige my function

i am the idea
when he needed one
molded from mud
he crawls inside

and cries
where he'll be felt
i keep him warm
fast, so not to smother
starve and lose shape

one night i wake to find him dead inside me
his carcass rotting, bloated and rancid
i carry him though his stink
marks my own
but to dump him aside
would make me hollow
filth is better than a vacuum
filth is existence
where a vacuum is
nonexistence

i am the record
of his appetite
played on repeat
broken
i am the kite
tethered to the storm
to take the blows
in proof of god
i am the stone
tomb hardened and cold
to keep myself
regressed, in hibernation
where i will not feel
or be felt
i fit each mold
i'm stuffed inside
servile piece
set in walls and stairwell steps
cobbled roads
castle spires
i do not disturb

i am multipurpose
genie in a toolbox
the locomotive
with no brakes
the mask
without a face
i am the mason's trowel
the potter's wheel
alchemist's scale
philosopher's pen
dumbwaiter
soothsayer
glass
elevator
i am the songbird
you bought
and wished
to be a real boy
for eros to lay bare his form
you did not expect
the bedrock to crack
our ruptured edifice
upon which a whole city
crumbled
beams
splintered
walls
toppled
hearths
buried beneath
barren beds
the smashed pot
crushed metal
childless bauble
voiceless pen
i am the wreckage heap
a mess of mud
reeking of death

and i turn back
to the serpent's mouth
gripping teeth
gaping maw
and in the darkness
no one
he is gone
the stone moved
the tomb emptied
and i am alone
facing myself
my own face
open and wanting
i open my mouth
swallow myself
whole
retch myself
out
repeating, repeating
i am the cage
i made
choking serpent
self-fulfilling
ouroboros

yet even so
they came to me
from where
i cannot say
they climb my face
in twos and threes
looking for scraps
and places where
grass grows
they take shelter
in my shadow
where i've kept the earth
rich and fertile
and crawl inside

the cavernous spaces
unafraid of the dark
i am still
unmoving, unchanging
yet i cower
at the warmth

passing seasons
pass and grow
these strange settlers
of the wreckage heap
purposeless ruin
in the winter they
sled my slopes
and carve out
niches in the snow
in spring they
collect the melt
cascading down the furrows
from my brow
in summer they
trace my paths
past shale and scree
shattered and splintered
remnant
and at the first turn
of autumn
they summit my peaks
and sing out hymns
to the aether
why sing?
who for?
unmoving, unchanging
i listen

they sing for birds
they sing for wind
they sing for laughter, and

me

they sing for me
and my jaw drops in awe
as i drop from my jaw
falling
faltering
growing
expanding outward
to meet these other things
to touch
to feel
breathless
torn open
wider and wider
too fast, too great
but not ever enough
and i feel the wind ripping through my chasms
and i feel the laughter rippling through my stones
and i feel the light trickling upward
in a gravity of its own make
from my roots
from the earth
and i begin to understand

from then on
i watch them grow
as i grow
their weight
the weight of my world
everchanging
in and out
with the ocean tide
in times of war
i give them trenches
in times of peace
i give them treasures
and when they are lost
or far from here

they look to that seam
between water and firmament
and mark me
sown to the world
needle of the compass
around which all light spins

for i am the mountain
who stands alone
but not alone
who has risen from mud
to swallow the sunrise
in all its flame
i burn the corpse
breathe out smoke
red heat
from my belly
they make sacrifices to me
for their harvest
and ask no more
for i am
only am
that is

hollowed, hallowed
home

* * *

over the course of my travels
i would often recall
one story in particular
of a young man
gangly and earnest
speeding alone
along a highway
desperate to get home
before midnight

on the verge of sleep
pedals pressed petals
twice past the limit
as i listened to
ennio morricone
to steady myself
the trumpet truly is
the voice of god
but our voices
are no fainter
got pulled over
in the midst of
l'estasi dell'oro
fiddled with the
bouquet as i
showed him your letter
avoided the ticket

two hours later
i pulled past the
hydrangeas at the
edge of the driveway
dragged myself
collapsed into
the bed you had made me
cotton and chamomile
you took my clothes
draped me in scent
jasmine in bloom

lily of my valley
i held you
the ecstasy of you
wanting to keep
that night
the night you asked me
to marry you

                        * * *

in later months play
a game of life
with family
cards set on the empty chair
sat next to me
i take it home
and rest it
by my windowsill
to summon a ghost
i don't believe in
my first dreamcatcher
my last prayer

                wake!   wake!
                                                      find you
                                      sleeping there
portrait
of the madonna in flesh
                    the night in orbit and wonder
                                    of you
                                  you
                            alight
                          on
                       my
                            mountain
           sower of seeds
   origin
                            feet bare
              hair burning silver
                                          skin
where your fingertips graze   springs brush
where your lips brush   breaks spring
                    flowers crest
                                 streams and pools swell
       and where you
           lay to rest
                           consecrated
                               ground
        from which   new   life   grows

        thus i feel you
    happiness the weight of
        sadness made of
            both of us
                                    you cry
                                        "merci
                                        les étoiles !"

and the stars name us

                    "eden"

                    * * *

pan spits
in my face
cook with gas on high
i tell a joke
that no one hears
as i wait
through the forgotten moments
before they arrive
in twos and threes
they take their seats
at the long table
one laughing body
and me the head
with a hundred eyes
turned inward
i catch the light
in a drinking glass
silent wonders
have i earned it?
can i deserve it?
a feast prepared
roast turkey, maple yams
green beans and pulled pork
emptied bottles of
cabernet;
on my plate i paint a pollock
and find a rose
of bread and apple slices
its petals fall way
pulled by their smiling eyes
licking like candle flames
set at an altar
which i envision
to one day seat millions
and we will flicker together

* * *

[a transcription in translation:]

you take many forms

                                                            oh?
                                      what form am i now?

a princess
a queen

                                             how beautiful

but not as beautiful
as the wind

                                             am i the wind?

yes
i think you always have been
crashing against my face
caressing the curls of my hair

                                                  (sigh)

you play with me
knock over my mug
blow away hats and tents and hesitation

                                            (giggles)

you rush forward undaunted
billowing out sails
your path clear and true

                                 i think you need some sleep

at times you're loud and boisterous
ringing bells out of tune
throwing swarms of leaves
roaring through my window

                                 i'm glad you can see it too

other times you're quiet and sheepish
afraid to enter the room
lest you disturb something

                                        i'll remember that

there are days where you storm and rage
where you upturn the earth and tear down trees
screaming through the living air

                              and i love you for tolerating it

and then there are days
where you aren't there anymore
you're off somewhere else
and i'm left alone

                                    but i always come back!
                                    i take many forms, yes,

                                                                     but so do we

yeah
i know

                       [you kissed me on my forehead
                                 and then
                            in an instant
                         you were gone]

                 * * *

how dull must be heaven
mundane paradise
to be a song without end
or a sun without rise
let me be banished
to wrestle with angels
and bleed my own eucharist
though we may try
past our expiration date
i hold the very passing as sacred
these shared passages with you
too worthy, too important
to have lasted forever

let us dance in the graveyard
until we drop dead
and when we die
let us expand outward
into memory
until even that fades
with the names on our stones
i speak your name now
hands cupped in devotion
to be gifted over the water
like ashes to the wind
like praises to the dusk

Thank you.
you who went to the grave
and pulled me along

Thank you.
you who bought me
who found me in the mud
and said i was her "everything"

Thank you.
you who saw
the mountain in the man

and decided to climb.

epilogue

she laces up her boots
smiles coyly at me as we
step out on kintsugi sidewalks
factories and churches
left in testament
of bygone blocks
we walked this path
long ago i think
but that time has evanesced
with the fading of our footsteps
on pavement

the things i remember and were no longer exist
the things you remember and were no longer exist
the things we remember and were no longer exist
the things we'll learn and be have yet to exist

window shopping
she chooses an antique store
labyrinth of furniture, books, clothing and
i spy a red bird
suspended on a string
like one point in a constellation
my mother had kept one
similar in the nursery
i feel the craftsmanship
between my fingers and
recall the cherokee tale
that the first cardinal
was the daughter of the sun
tragically slain
before her wedding day
a group of warriors tasked
to bring her back
from the country of the dead
failed their instruction
but unlike the elegy
of eurydice
a verse of hers did

make the journey
and all who heard
its chirruping melody
recognized it as
enough
all we can ask for
all we can give

she takes my hand
and leads me onward
checkout line
cashier is new
we buy a crib
along with the mobile

acknowledgments

The following poems originally appeared, titled and sometimes in different versions, in the publications listed below:

Anthropocene: pages 35-37 (under the title "flight from fairy land"), page 62 (under the title "eucharist"), and pages 65-66 (under the title "wedding vows").

Eunoia Review: page 3 (under the title "chorus"), pages 7-8 (under the title "i walk the desert desolate"), page 9 (under the title "instruction"), pages 30-31 (under the title "in exile"), pages 32-34 (under the title "kosmogonia"), and page 50 (under the title "the next morning").

Rising Phoenix Review: pages 25-26 (under the title "the curse").

I'd like to thank everyone who, directly or indirectly, helped in the making of this book. Thanks to Joe Weil, whose essay *Toward a more Combative and Passionate Reading of Poems* was the inspiration I needed to use the name given me and wrestle with angels. Thanks to Anagh Banerjee, who blessed my work with more art and beauty than it was worth (I remember well our conversation on the life of places). Thanks to Harry Shapiro, who stepped up when a friend needed him most, Michael Broder and the Indolent Books team, who through it all believed in these poems, and Ashley McGregor, who got me to return to these poems in the first place. Thanks to all the wonderful poets, editors and friends who first read and supported my work; and above all thanks to my family, who with their light showed me the way.

Jacob David Snyder is a freelance writer and editor. His work has been featured in the journals *Anthropocene*, *Eunoia Review*, and *Rising Phoenix Review*, and in the variety show *Hottie Bop*. He's contributed to the production of several publications, including *Poems in the Aftermath: An Anthology from the 2016 Presidential Transition Period*, by Indolent Books, and *The Beginner's Guide to Manga and Anime*, by Scholastic. He lives in New York City.

www.ingramcontent.com/pod-product-compliance
Lightning Source LLC
Chambersburg PA
CBHW022120090426
42743CB00008B/930